GOAT: Women in Sports

Caitlin Clark

College Basketball GOAT

HOT TOPICS

Gareth Stevens PUBLISHING

BY KRISTEN RAJCZAK NELSON

Please visit our website, www.garethstevens.com. For a free color catalog of all our high-quality books, call toll free 1-800-542-2595 or fax 1-877-542-2596.

Cataloging-in-Publication Data
Names: Rajczak Nelson, Kristen.
Title: Caitlin Clark: college basketball GOAT / Kristen Rajczak Nelson.
Description: Buffalo, NY : Gareth Stevens Publishing, 2025. | Series: GOAT: women in sports | Includes glossary and index.
Identifiers: ISBN 9781482470512 (pbk.) | ISBN 9781482470529 (library bound) | ISBN 9781482470536 (ebook)
Subjects: LCSH: Women basketball players–United States–Biography–Juvenile literature. | Women athletes–United States–Biography–Juvenile literature. | Women's National Basketball Association–Juvenile literature. | Indiana Fever (Basketball team)--History–Juvenile literature. | Guards (Basketball)–United States–Biography–Juvenile literature.
Classification: LCC GV884.A1 R33 2025 | DDC 796.323092 B–dc23

First Edition

Published in 2025 by
Gareth Stevens Publishing
2544 Clinton St
Buffalo, NY 14224

Designer: Leslie Taylor
Editor: Kristen Rajczak Nelson

Photo credits: Cover, pp. 7, 29 (photo) ZUMA Press, Inc./Alamy.com, (wreath) Igoron_vector_3D_render/Shutterstock.com, (banner, cover & series background) RETHELD DESIGN IRI/Shutterstock.com, (basketball icon) Invision Frame/Shutterstock.com; p. 5 John Mac/File:230303 JohnMc IA Purdue 90.jpg_commons.wikimedia.org; pp. 9, 15, 25, 27 ASSOCIATED PRESS/newsroom.ap.org; p. 11 MGoBlog/File:Caitlin Clark (2).jpg_commons.wikimedia.org; p. 12 FIBA/File:2018wbbwclogo.png_commons.wikimedia.org; p. 13 230303 JohnMc_IA_Purdue_67/flickr.com; p. 17 Sipa USA/Alamy.com; p. 19 John Mac/File:Caitlin Clark Big Ten tournament 2 (cropped).jpg_commons.wikimedia.org; p. 21 UPI/Alamy.com; p. 23 State Farm_ Iowa Basketball guard Caitlin Clark shows off her new khakis with Jake from State Farm/Flickr.com.

Printed in the United States of America

Some of the images in this book illustrate individuals who are models. The depictions do not imply actual situations or events.

CPSIA compliance information: Batch #CSGS25: For further information contact Gareth Stevens, New York, New York at 1-800-542-2595.

Contents

Superstar

After an incredible senior season at the University of Iowa, Caitlin Clark is unquestionably the GOAT—greatest of all time—of college basketball. But this driven, talented player doesn't want to stop there. She wants to be a basketball **legend**!

WHAT A STAR!

Early in the 2023–2024 season, Caitlin told *ESPN*: "I have to be the best **version** of myself for my teammates, and for the fans, and for my family."

Iowa Beginnings

Caitlin was born on January 22, 2002. She grew up in West Des Moines, Iowa, with an older brother named Blake and a younger brother named Colin. Much of her family is **athletic**. Caitlin started playing sports very young.

CAITLIN WITH HER PARENTS, ANNE AND BRENT

WHAT A STAR!

Caitlin and her brothers used to play basketball in the basement and on the driveway when they were growing up.

Caitlin played softball, tennis, golf, and other sports as a child. Caitlin's dad was one of her first basketball coaches. As Caitlin's basketball talent really started to show, she played on boys' teams. She was also a great soccer player!

WHAT A STAR!

Caitlin has always been competitive, or had a drive to win. She used to cry after every game she lost as a kid!

Taking Over the Court

Caitlin went to Dowling Catholic High School. At first, she played both basketball and soccer. She was the leading scorer on the soccer team! Then, she made basketball her main sport. The team went to the state **tournament** three times with Caitlin on the court.

WHAT A STAR!

On February 4, 2019, Caitlin scored 60 points in a game as a junior at Dowling Catholic!

Caitlin often got upset when a play didn't go how she wanted. She sometimes yelled at teammates. Still, she became one of the all-time high scorers in Iowa girls' basketball history. Many colleges **recruited** her. Caitlin chose to play for the University of Iowa Hawkeyes.

FIBA WOMEN'S BASKETBALL WORLD CUP

WHAT A STAR!

Caitlin won a gold medal with the Team USA under-19 women's team at the World Cup in 2019! She won another gold with the team in 2021.

Hawkeye Start

Caitlin started at Iowa in fall 2020. Even though she was just a freshman, she was the starting point guard from her first practice. Caitlin **expected** a lot from her new teammates. When they didn't deliver, Caitlin showed her anger.

WHAT A STAR!

As a freshman, Caitlin led the National Collegiate Athletic Association (NCAA) **Division 1** women's teams in scoring and assists.

Caitlin is known for taking long three-point shots. These started to be her **signature** move during her second year playing with Iowa. Caitlin made such a big impact that season that she was named University of Iowa Women's Athlete of the Year!

WHAT A STAR!

Caitlin led the Hawkeyes to win their division (Big Ten) tournament in 2022. She was named Big Ten player of the year too.

Winning Mindset

As the 2022–2023 season started, Caitlin was working on her attitude on the court. She adopted a saying: "Find peace in the quest." Her work paid off in a winning season. She scored a buzzer-beating three-point shot to win the last regular season game!

WHAT A STAR!

Caitlin won many awards her junior year, including Naismith Women's College Player of the Year, Associated Press Women's College Basketball Player of the Year, and Big Ten Female Athlete of the Year!

Caitlin and the Hawkeyes again won the Big Ten Tournament. They went into the NCAA tournament with high hopes. They went all the way to the championship game! Caitlin scored 30 points—but the Hawkeyes lost to Louisiana State University.

WHAT A STAR!

After the game, Caitlin said: "I understand we came up one win short, but I think we have a lot to be proud of and a lot to celebrate. I was just that young girl, so all you have to do is dream, and you can be in moments like this."

Record Breaker

Caitlin led the Hawkeyes to a winning season in 2023–2024. She averaged 31.6 points a game! She also did something more incredible. She broke the NCAA women's **career** scoring record! The shot that broke the record was one of Caitlin's signature threes from 30 feet (9.1 m).

WHAT A STAR!

Caitlin became such a big star that companies like State Farm, Gatorade, and Nike signed her to deals that made her millions of dollars!

Caitlin then broke the NCAA men's career scoring record! This made her the highest-scoring D1 college basketball player ever. Caitlin and the Hawkeyes followed this with a run that led them to another NCAA championship game. They lost to South Carolina.

WHAT A STAR!

About 18.7 million people watched the 2024 women's basketball championship game. This was in part because everyone wanted to see Caitlin play!

No. 1 Pick

Caitlin could have played one more year of college basketball. Instead, she declared she would be part of the Women's National Basketball Association (WNBA) **draft**. In April 2024, Caitlin was chosen first by the Indiana Fever!

WHAT A STAR!

After the Fever chose Caitlin, her jersey became the best-selling jersey of a draft pick ever on popular sports clothing website Fanatics.

Legend in the Making

Caitlin's journey from NCAA superstar to WNBA player has just begun! Her drive, skill, and love of the game are likely to take her far on both the national and world stage. What will she accomplish next?

WHAT A STAR!

Through the Caitlin Clark Foundation, Caitlin works to help young people and their communities in many ways, including through sports programs.

Caitlin Clark BY THE NUMBERS

Height: 6 feet (1.8 m)

Jersey number: 22

Draft pick: 1

NCAA career points: 3,951

Three-point shots made in the NCAA: 548

NCAA games played: 139

30-point games: 59

40-point games: 13

For More Information

BOOKS

Flynn, Brendan. *The History of Basketball.* Minneapolis, MN: Jump! Inc., 2025.

Tischler, Joe. *A'Ja Wilson.* Mankato, MN: Amicus Learning, 2025.

WEBSITES

Caitlin Clark
caitlinclark22.com
Keep up with everything Caitlin is doing on her website.

Caitlin Clark Foundation
caitlinclarkfoundation.org
Find out more about how Caitlin is making the world a better place.

Publisher's note to educators and parents: Our editors have carefully reviewed these websites to ensure that they are suitable for students. Many websites change frequently, however, and we cannot guarantee that a site's future contents will continue to meet our high standards of quality and educational value. Be advised that students should be closely supervised whenever they access the internet.

Glossary

athletic: Having to do with skill in sports.

career: The period of time an athlete spends playing a sport.

Division 1: The top division, or part, of the NCAA.

draft: The process of selecting new players from a pool of potential players entering the league.

expect: To think that something is likely to happen.

legend: A person who is well-known for doing something very well.

recruit: To find a person and try to get them to join a team.

signature: Something that is closely tied to a person.

tournament: A series of contests testing the skill of many athletes in the same sport.

version: A form of something that is different from others.

Index